GOAL!

By Mark Woods and Ruth Owen

Gareth Stevens
Publishing

GOAL!

By Mark Woods and Ruth Owen

Gareth Stevens
Publishing

Please visit our Web site, www.garethstevens.com. For a free color catalog of all our high-quality books, call toll free 1-800-542-2595 or fax 1-877-542-2596.

Library of Congress Cataloging-in-Publication Data

Woods, Mark.
Goal! : soccer facts and stats / Mark Woods and Ruth Owen.
   p. cm. — (Top score math)
ISBN 978-1-4339-5015-5 (library binding)
1. Soccer—Juvenile literature. 2. Soccer—Mathematics—Juvenile literature. I. Owen, Ruth, 1967- II. Title.
GV943.25.W65 2011
796.334—dc22

                  2010029686

Published in 2011 by
Gareth Stevens Publishing
111 East 14th Street, Suite 349
New York, NY 10003

© Ruby Tuesday Books Limited 2010

Developed & Created by Ruby Tuesday Books Ltd

Project Director – Ruth Owen
Designer – Alix Wood
Editor – Ben Hubbard
Consultants – Sally Smith, Hilary Koll, and Steve Mills
© Ruby Tuesday Books Limited 2010

Images: Getty front cover (Michael Regan), title page (Lars Baron), 6–7 (Jewel Samad), 7 top (Lui Jin), 8 (Guang Niu), 9 (Darren England), 10 left (Tony Duffy), 10 right (Popperfoto), 11 (Bob Thomas), 12–13 (Vincent Amalvy), 14 left (Robert Amora), 14–15 (Mike Hewitt), 16 (Lluis Gene), 17 (Paul Ellis), 20 (Rolls Press), 24–25 (Laurence Griffiths), 26 (Neil Jones), 28 (Marty Melville). Shutterstock 18, 19, 23 bottom. Wikipedia (public domain) 22, 23 top, 24 bottom.

While every effort has been made to secure permission to use copyright material, the publishers apologize for any errors or omissions in the above list and would be grateful for notification of any corrections to be included in subsequent editions.

Printed in the United States of America

CPSIA compliance information: Batch #CW11GS: For further information contact Gareth Stevens, New York, New York at 1-800-542-2595.

CONTENTS

WHAT WAS THE SCORE?

"What was the score?" It's the first question everyone asks when you say, "I went to the game." Then you talk about wins, losses, and points. It all adds up over the season.

Soccer was developed in England over 150 years ago. The first set of official rules was created at Cambridge University in 1848.

Numbers aren't just on the backs of the players' shirts in soccer. They help us follow the action – whether it's the school team or the World Cup. Numbers also allow managers to calculate when their side is doing well or badly.

Soccer is played between two teams of 11 players, and a game lasts 90 minutes. The side that scores the most goals wins the match.

Being good at soccer takes practice. It's the same with numbers. When you practice your math skills, you improve your math fitness.

Birgit Prinz

Birgit Prinz of Germany has scored a record 14 goals in World Cup finals. Kristine Lilly of the USA and Bente Nordby of Norway have both appeared in five World Cup finals.

Spain celebrate winning the 2010 World Cup Final in South Africa.

Hundreds of millions of people around the world watch the World Cup on TV. Representing your country at the World Cup is the biggest honor a soccer player can have.

Let's get started!

RECORD BREAKERS

There have been some record-breaking games, goals, and achievements in soccer.

53

In 2010, Glasgow Rangers won the Scottish League Championship for the 53rd time. No other club in the world has won their national title more times.

149

The largest win in a match was set in Madagascar in 2002. A team named AS Adema beat their biggest rivals SO L'Emyrne 149–0. The L'Emyrne players were unhappy at a referee's decision, so they kept kicking the ball into their own net!

340

Kristine Lilly is a midfielder for the USA women's team. By 2008, she had earned 340 caps.

Kristine Lilly (in white) in action in the 2007 World Cup.

Goalkeeper Mohamed Al-Deayea of Saudi Arabia has made the most international appearances for his country. Between 1990 and 2006, he played in goal 181 times.

181

31

The largest win in an international game happened in a 2001 World Cup qualifier. Australia beat American Samoa 31–0. Australian player Archie Thompson (above) set his own record by scoring 13 of the goals!

Try answering these quiz questions about record-breaking soccer facts and statistics.

1) Look at the numbers in the red circles. Which number is:
   a) **10 x 34**
   b) **208 ÷ 4 + 1**
   c) **75 + 38 + 68**
   d) **88 – 57**
   e) **120 + 80 – 51**

2) The biggest-ever crowd to watch a women's soccer match was **90,185** spectators. The match was the 1999 World Cup Final between the USA and China. Write the number **90,185** in words.

3) Real Madrid has won the European Cup/Champions League a record nine times. Which of these numbers are multiples of 9?

   27   47   18   90   82   59

4) In 2008, Kristine Lilly reached a record-breaking 340 caps.
   a) Divide 340 by 10
   b) Multiply 340 by 10
   c) Divide 340 by 100

5) How many calculations can you make in five minutes using the numbers in the red circles? Here's one to get you started:
   31 + 340 + 53 = 424

BLAST FROM THE PAST

Soccer has become the most popular sport in the world. The names of some of soccer's top stars are known worldwide. Here are just three of soccer's best players from history.

PELÉ

Pelé's real name is Edison Arantes do Nascimento. He won three World Cup medals with Brazil and became one of the most famous sportsmen ever.

Date of birth: October 23, 1940
Clubs:
Santos 1956–1974
New York Cosmos 1975–1977
International team: Brazil
Number of caps: 92
International goals: 77
World Cup competitions:
1958, 1962, 1966, 1970

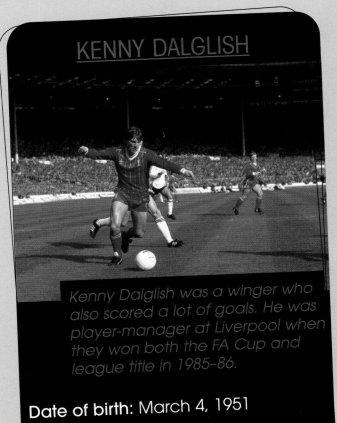

KENNY DALGLISH

Kenny Dalglish was a winger who also scored a lot of goals. He was player-manager at Liverpool when they won both the FA Cup and league title in 1985–86.

Date of birth: March 4, 1951
Clubs:
Celtic 1969–1977
Liverpool 1977–1990
International team: Scotland
Number of caps: 102
International goals: 30
World Cup competitions:
1974, 1978, 1982

DIEGO MARADONA

Diego Maradona is remembered for scoring amazing goals and leading Argentina to win the 1986 World Cup.

Date of birth: October 30, 1960
Clubs:
Argentinos Juniors 1976–1981
Boca Juniors 1981–1982
Barcelona 1982–1984
Napoli 1984–1991
Sevilla 1992–1993
Newell's Old Boys 1993–1994
Boca Juniors 1995–1997
International team: Argentina
Number of caps: 91
International goals: 34
World Cup competitions:
1982, 1986, 1990, 1994

BLAST FROM THE PAST QUIZ

Try answering these quiz questions using the players' facts and statistics.

1) Look at the players' club information.
   a) Which club did Pelé play for in 1963?
   b) Which clubs did Diego Maradona play for in 1993?
   c) Which club did Kenny Dalglish play for in 1980?

2) Who is the oldest of the three great players?

3) Work out the difference in international goals between these players.
   a) Pelé and Maradona
   b) Pelé and Kenny Dalglish
   c) Kenny Dalglish and Maradona

4) Kenny Dalglish played in **938** games in his career. Which of these numbers is closest to **938**?

   893   988   983   899   833

5) The three great players earned **102, 92,** and **91** caps in their careers. Here are three sequences that begin with those numbers. Find the missing numbers in each sequence.

   a) **102   104   ?   108   110   ?   114**
   b) **92   102   ?   122   132   ?   152**
   c) **91   100   ?   118   127   ?   145**

The FIFA World Cup is the biggest international soccer tournament in the world. The best 32 men's national teams in the world play in the men's World Cup finals. In the FIFA Women's World Cup, the best 16 women's teams take part.

WORLD CUP WINNERS

	Winner	Score	Runner-up
1930	Uruguay	4–2	Argentina
1934	Italy	2–1	Czechoslovakia
1938	Italy	4–2	Hungary
1950	Uruguay	2–1	Brazil
1954	West Germany	3–2	Hungary
1958	Brazil	5–2	Sweden
1962	Brazil	3–1	Czechoslovakia
1966	England	4–2	West Germany
1970	Brazil	4–1	Italy
1974	West Germany	2–1	Netherlands
1978	Argentina	3–1	Netherlands
1982	Italy	3–1	West Germany
1986	Argentina	3–2	West Germany
1990	West Germany	1–0	Argentina
1994	Brazil	0–0*	Italy
1998	France	3–0	Brazil
2002	Brazil	2–0	Germany
2006	Italy	1–1*	France
2010	Spain	1–0	Netherlands

* Decided on penalties

Two players have appeared in five World Cup finals. The players are Mexico's Antonio Carbajal and Germany's Lothar Matthäus.

Ronaldo of Brazil has scored 15 goals in World Cup finals (1998–2006). Here, he shoots and scores in the 2002 World Cup Final between Brazil and Germany.

WORLD CUP QUIZ

Try these quiz questions about the World Cup.

1) The FIFA Women's World Cup has been played every four years since 1991. Can you fill in the missing Women's World Cup years in this sequence?

1991   1995   ?   2003   ?

2) Look at the **Winner** column in the **World Cup Winners** chart. How many times has each of the winning teams won the competition?

3) Brazil has played in seven World Cup Final matches. How many goals did Brazil score in total in those games?

4) The green chart shows some of the knock-out stages of a World Cup.

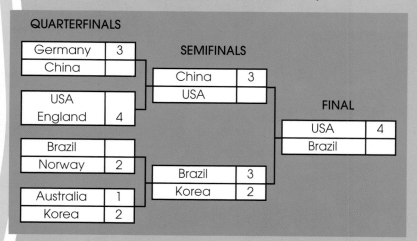

QUARTERFINALS

| Germany | 3 |
| China | |

| USA | |
| England | 4 |

| Brazil | |
| Norway | 2 |

| Australia | 1 |
| Korea | 2 |

SEMIFINALS

| China | 3 |
| USA | |

| Brazil | 3 |
| Korea | 2 |

FINAL

| USA | 4 |
| Brazil | |

Use the statements below to help you fill in the missing numbers in the chart.
 • In the quarterfinals, each winning team scored one goal more than their opponent.
 • The USA scored 13 goals in total.
 • Brazil scored 11 goals in total.

5) Who won the tournament?

SOCCER LEAGUES

Almost every country has a national league to decide who is the best team. Every club and player wants to get to the top of the league by gaining the most points during the season. After every match, you can calculate your team's position and whether your team is heading up or down in the league!

Chelsea (blue) vs Arsenal

PREMIER LEAGUE
England
Start: 1992
Major clubs:
Manchester United, Chelsea, Liverpool, Arsenal

LA Galaxy vs New York Red Bulls

MAJOR LEAGUE SOCCER
USA/Canada
Start: 1993
Major clubs: LA Galaxy, New York Red Bulls, Houston Dynamo

LEAGUES QUIZ

Have fun trying these quiz questions about league tables.

In a league, the teams win points to obtain their position in the league from top to bottom. The results of each game are recorded in a league table.

All the teams in this league have played four games.

	P	W	D	L	F	A	GD	PTS
1 City	4	3	1	0	7	4	+3	10
2 United	4	2	1	1	7	3	+4	7
3 Rovers	4	1	1	2	6	8	-2	4
4 Rangers	4	0	1	3	1	6	-5	1

LEAGUE TABLE KEY

P = Played

W = Win

D = Draw

L = Loss

F = Goals scored for

A = Goals scored against

GD = The goal difference between F and A

PTS = Points earned

Here is the points system:
- **Win = 3 points**
- **Draw = 1 point**
- **Loss = 0 points**

To decide which team is best, we first look at total points (PTS). If two teams are even on points, then we can look at their goal difference (GD).

1) Here are the results for Week 5 of the league.
   Rovers 2–0 United
   City 1–1 Rangers
   Draw the league table above in a notebook.
   Now update the table with the Week 5 results.

2) After Week 5, which teams are in 2nd and 3rd place?

3) Now update your table with the Week 6 results.
   United 0–1 City
   Rangers 1–3 Rovers

4) Which team has 10 points after Week 6?

5) What are the positions in the league after Week 6?

RIVALS!

Rivalries are an important part of club soccer. Rivals are two teams who have a long history of playing against each other and wanting badly to win. When they meet, it matters more than any other game! Let's look at two famous soccer rivalries.

When Real Madrid and Barcelona meet up, the game is known as "El Clasico."

(Statistics to May 2010)	REAL MADRID	BARCELONA
Stadium:	Bernabeu Capacity: 80,354	Camp Nou Capacity 98,772
League titles:	31	20
Spanish Cups:	17	25
European Cups/ Champions League:	9	3
Head-to-head wins:	68	64

Real Madrid's Cristiano Ronaldo shoots against Barcelona.

No player has been transferred between Manchester United and Liverpool since 1964!

Liverpool celebrates scoring against their rivals Manchester United in a Premier League match.

SOCCER RIVALS QUIZ

Use the teams' facts and statistics to answer these quiz questions.

1) What's the difference?
   a) Real Madrid and Barcelona league titles.
   b) Manchester United and Liverpool FA cups.
   c) Real Madrid and Barcelona Spanish Cups.

2) Real Madrid and Barcelona play each other 30 more times. Real Madrid wins 18 of the games and Barcelona wins 12. What are the new head-to-head wins totals for each club?

3) Manchester United and Liverpool are playing each other at Anfield. If 28,050 United fans want to go to the game and 17,375 Liverpool fans want to go, how many fans won't get in?

4) If the same match is played at Old Trafford, how many spare places will there be?

5) In 1943, Real Madrid beat Barcelona 11–1. Look at this sequence of match scores. Can you see a pattern? Fill in the missing numbers.

11–1   10–2   9–3   ?   7–5   ?

(Statistics to May 2010)	MANCHESTER UNITED	LIVERPOOL
Stadium:	Old Trafford	Anfield
	Capacity: 76,212	Capacity: 45,362
League titles:	18	18
FA Cups:	11	7
European Cups/ Champions League:	3	5
Head-to-head wins:	69	60

Manchester United and Liverpool soccer clubs are just 30 miles apart. When they meet, it is known as the "North-West derby."

COMPARE THE STARS

Cristiano Ronaldo and Wayne Rooney are two of the most exciting strikers in the world. They used to be teammates at Manchester United where they had a lot of success in the English Premier League and in the European Champions League. But who is the better player?

WAYNE ROONEY
Nationality: English
Date of birth: October 24, 1985
Clubs: Everton 2002–2004
Manchester United 2004
English Premier League wins:
2007, 2008, 2009
UEFA Champions League: 2008

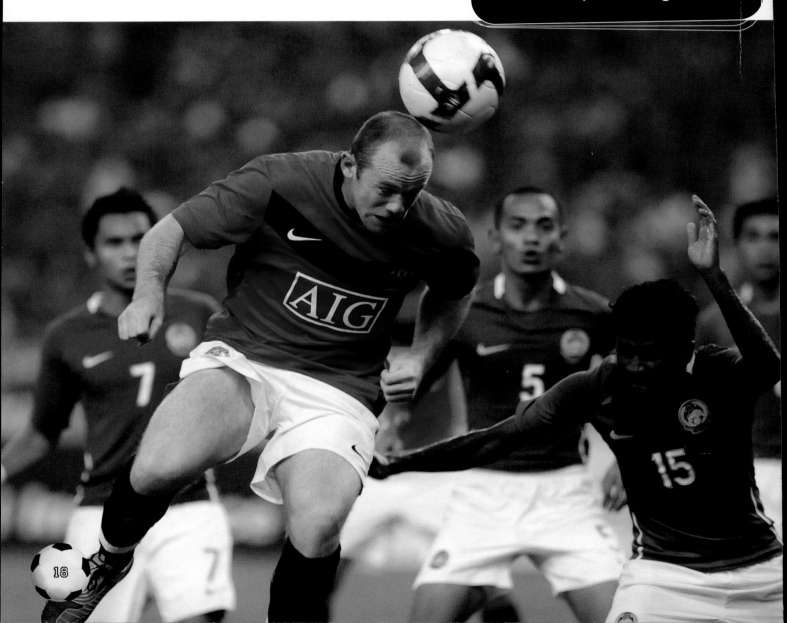

SOCCER STARS QUIZ

Try these soccer stars quiz questions.

1) Who is the older of the two players? By how many days is he the older?

PLAYER STATISTICS

Season	CRISTIANO RONALDO		WAYNE ROONEY	
	Played	Goals	Played	Goals
2002–2003	31	5	37	8
2003–2004	40	6	40	9
2004–2005	50	9	43	17
2005–2006	47	12	48	19
2006–2007	53	23	55	23
2007–2008	49	42	43	18
2008–2009	53	26	49	20

Use the **Player Statistics** chart above to answer these questions.

2) Which player scored more goals in the 2005–2006 season?

3) a) How many games did Ronaldo play in total?
   b) How many games did Rooney play in total?

4) In which seasons did the players have the following goal differences?
   a) 8   b) 24   c) 7

5) Which player scored more goals than the other between 2002 and 2009? How many more goals did he score?

CRISTIANO RONALDO
Nationality: Portuguese
Date of birth: February 5, 1985
Clubs: Sporting Lisbon
2001–2003
Manchester United 2003–2009
Real Madrid 2009
English Premier League wins:
2007, 2008, 2009
FA Cup: 2004
UEFA Champions League: 2008

BRAZIL IS THE BEST

Brazil has won the World Cup five times. The Brazilian team of 1970 is considered the greatest side ever. This team mixed skill, huge talent, and an attacking approach that won them fans all over the world!

Brazil meets Italy in the 1970 World Cup Final

BRAZIL 1970 WORLD CUP RESULTS

Group Stage Games
- England 1–0 Romania
- Brazil 4–1 Czechoslovakia
- Romania 2–1 Czechoslovakia
- Brazil 1–0 England
- Brazil 3–2 Romania
- England 1–0 Czechoslovakia

Quarterfinals
- Brazil 4–2 Peru

Semifinals
- Brazil 3–1 Uruguay

Final
- Brazil 4–1 Italy

Pelé and Mário Zagallo are the only two players to win three World Cup medals. Pelé won his medals in 1958, 1962, and 1970. Mário Zagallo was Pelé's teammate in 1958 and 1962, and he was the team manager in 1970!

Now try these quiz questions.

1) Look at the **Brazil 1970 World Cup Results** list. Use the group stage results to complete the World Cup table below. We have filled in England's results to get you started.

WORLD CUP TABLE KEY

P = Played
W = Win
D = Draw
L = Loss
F = Goals scored for
A = Goals scored against
GD = The goal difference between F and A
PTS = Points earned

	P	W	D	L	F	A	GD	PTS
Brazil								
England	3	2	0	1	2	1	+1	4
Romania								
Czechoslovakia								

• **Win = 2 points** • **Draw = 1 point**

2) How many goals did Brazil score in the whole competition?

3) Between 1930 and 2010, Brazil scored 210 goals in World Cup final tournaments. Write this number in words.

4) Brazil is the only team to have qualified and played in every World Cup final from 1930 to 2010 – that's 19 competitions.
   a) Half of 19 is?
   b) 5 x 19 is?
   c) 19 minus 27 is?
   d) Nineteen multiplied by ten is?

5) Look at the **Shirt Numbers** box. Is each statement true or false?

SHIRT NUMBERS

a) 398 > 389
b) 658 < 685
c) 0.78 > 0.8
d) 0.5 < 0.05
e) 883 > 838
f) 0.25 > 0.20

STADIUMS

For most soccer fans, nothing beats watching a soccer match live with thousands of other supporters. Soccer fans can watch games in huge stadiums around the world.

Estádio do Maracanã

In 1950, over 199,000 fans watched Brazil play Uruguay in the World Cup Final at the Estádio do Maracanã.

STADIUM FACTS

Name	Country	Opened	Capacity
Rungrado May Day Stadium	North Korea	1989	150,000
Estádio do Maracanã	Brazil	1950	82,238
Soccer City	South Africa	1989	94,700
Salt Lake Stadium	India	1984	120,000
Estadio Azteca	Mexico	1966	105,000
Red Bull Arena	USA	2010	25,189
Wembley Stadium	England	2007	90,000
Stadium Australia	Australia	1999	83,500

Soccer City in South Africa is the largest stadium in Africa. It was upgraded and improved for the 2010 World Cup. The outside is designed to look like a traditional African pot.

The new Wembley Stadium in London cost $1.25 billion to build. It replaced the old Wembley Stadium that had been on the same site for the previous 80 years.

STADIUMS QUIZ

Answer these quiz questions about stadiums.

1) Look at the **Stadium Facts** chart. Which of the stadiums could host a match for 95,000 fans?

2) Put the stadiums in order according to their capacity starting with the lowest.

3) Imagine this circle is a stadium divided into sections. Each section holds 2,500 fans. What is the stadium's capacity?

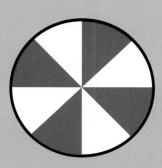

a)

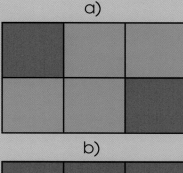

b)

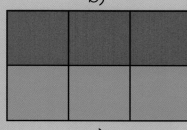

c)

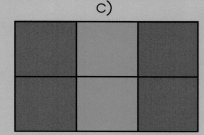

These diagrams represent the Salt Lake Stadium in India on three Saturdays. The red areas are filled to capacity with fans.

4) What fraction of the stadium is full on each Saturday?

5) If the Salt Lake Stadium holds 120,000 fans, how many fans are in the stadium on each Saturday?

23

SOCCER MONEY

Soccer managers can buy and sell players to create a winning squad. If a player has a contract with one team but moves to another, the two clubs agree on a transfer fee. Building a top soccer team can cost millions of dollars!

TRANSFER FEES
Transfer fees are getting bigger and bigger...

Year	Name	From	To	Transfer fee
1893	Willie Groves	West Bromwich Albion	Aston Villa	$157
1922	Syd Puddefoot	West Ham Utd	Falkirk	$7,825
1973	Johan Cruyff	Ajax	Barcelona	$1.44 million
1976	Paolo Rossi	Juventus	Vicenza	$2.74 million
1984	Diego Maradona	Barcelona	Napoli	$7.83 million
1990	Roberto Baggio	Fiorentina	Juventus	$12.52 million
1997	Ronaldo	Barcelona	Inter Milan	$30.53 million
1999	Christian Vieri	Lazio	Inter Milan	$50.1 million
2001	Zinedine Zidane	Juventus	Real Madrid	$72 million
2009	Cristiano Ronaldo	Manchester Utd	Real Madrid	$125.23 million

In 1905, English striker Alf Common moved from Sunderland to close rivals Middlesbrough for $1,565. In 1905, that was a world record!

Cristiano Ronaldo cost Real Madrid $125.23 million in 2009!

SOCCER MONEY QUIZ

Try these quiz questions about soccer's millions.

Look at this list of transfer fees:

Kaká	**$87.66 million**
Denilson	**$33.66 million**
Alan Shearer	**$23.48 million**
Christian Vieri	**$50 million**
Zinedine Zidane	**$72 million**
Luis Figo	**$58 million**

1) You buy Vieri, Denilson, and Figo. How much do you spend?

2) You sell Zidane and Kaká. How much money do you have?

3) You sell Denilson and Shearer. You want to buy Vieri and Figo. How much extra money will you need?

4) You have $137.75 million. Work out which combinations of players you can buy.

5) Can you match the six players and their transfer fees above to the bars on the **Transfer Fees Bar Chart**?

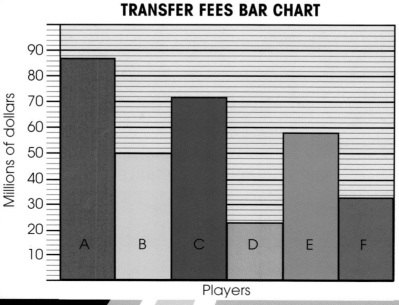

TRANSFER FEES BAR CHART

Millions of dollars

Players

SOCCER TRAINING

At training sessions, soccer managers and their assistants make sure everyone practices their shooting, passing, and defending every day.

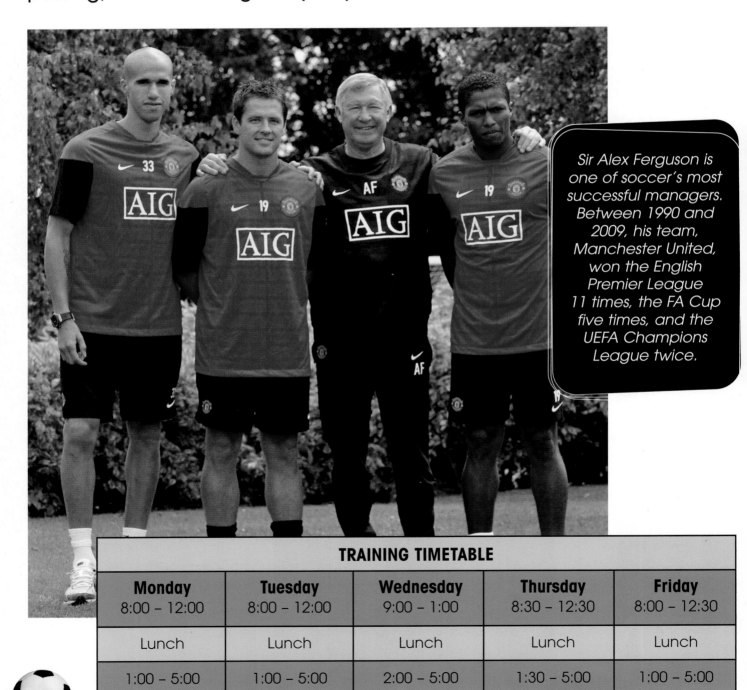

Sir Alex Ferguson is one of soccer's most successful managers. Between 1990 and 2009, his team, Manchester United, won the English Premier League 11 times, the FA Cup five times, and the UEFA Champions League twice.

TRAINING TIMETABLE				
Monday 8:00 – 12:00	**Tuesday** 8:00 – 12:00	**Wednesday** 9:00 – 1:00	**Thursday** 8:30 – 12:30	**Friday** 8:00 – 12:30
Lunch	Lunch	Lunch	Lunch	Lunch
1:00 – 5:00	1:00 – 5:00	2:00 – 5:00	1:30 – 5:00	1:00 – 5:00

KICK ABOUT ANGLES

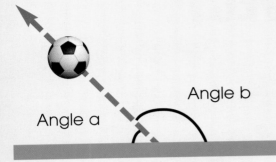

Angle b

Angle a

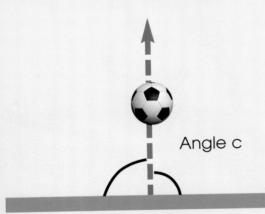

Angle c

135°

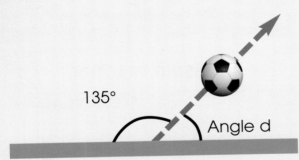

Angle d

Angle e

30°

Try these quiz questions about training.

Look at the **Training Timetable**.

1) How many hours of training will there be on Thursday?

2) How many minutes of training will there be on Friday morning?

3) How many hours of training will there be this week in total?

4) On Tuesday, the training plan is:
   2 hours of fitness training
   1.5 hours of passing practice
   75 minutes of defending practice
   75 minutes of free kicks practice
   30 minutes of running
   How long is left for practicing penalties?

5) Getting the angle right when you're shooting or passing is important.
   Take a look at the **Kick About Angles** and try these questions:
   a) What types of angle are a and b?
   b) How many degrees is angle c? What is this type of angle called?
   c) What is the size of angle d?
   d) What is the size of angle e?

PRACTICE MAKES PERFECT

Professional soccer players practice and practice their skills. During practice sessions, they work out a plan to beat their next opponent.

David Beckham practices free kicks during a training session with LA Galaxy.

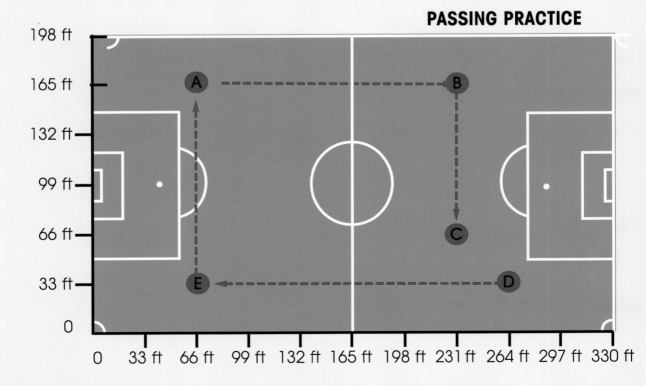

PASSING PRACTICE

DEFENDING PRACTICE

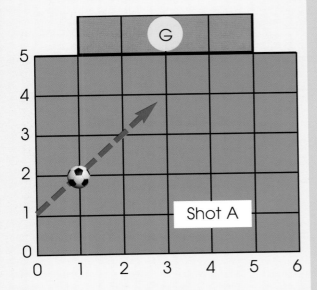

Shot A

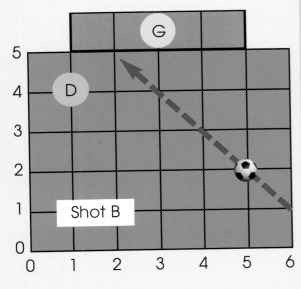

Shot B

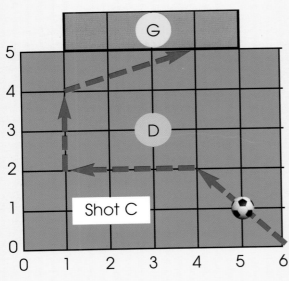

Shot C

PRACTICE MAKES PERFECT QUIZ

Can you answer these final quiz questions?

1) Look at the **Passing Practice** soccer pitch.
   The players are passing the ball.
   How long is each pass?
   a) Player A to Player B   b) Player B to Player C
   c) Player D to Player E   d) Player E to Player A

2) a) What is the perimeter of the **Passing Practice** soccer pitch?
   b) What is the area of the pitch?

Now look at the **Defending Practice** diagrams.
Each shot has been plotted on a grid map.

3) Look at **Shot A**. The goalie must move
   to block the shot. At which of these
   grid coordinates could the goalie block
   the shot?
   (2,5) (3,4) (5,5) (3,5) (4,5)

4) Look at **Shot B**.
   a) At which of these grid coordinates
      could the defender (D) block the shot?
      (4,3) (4,4) (2,4) (3,4) (3,3)
   b) If the goalie (G) moves to grid
      coordinates **(2,5)**, will he block the shot?

5) Look at **Shot C**.
   a) The red arrows show the path of the
      ball as the strikers try to set up a shot.
      At which of these grid coordinates
      could the defender (D) intercept
      the ball?
      (4,2) (2,3) (1,3) (3,4) (2,2) (1,4)
   b) At which of these grid coordinates
      could the goalie block the shot?
      (3,4) (1,4) (5,4) (4,5) (2,5)

9 RECORD BREAKERS QUIZ
1 a) 340 b) 53 c) 181
  d) 31 e) 149
2 Ninety thousand one hundred eighty-five
3 27 18 90
4 a) 34 b) 3,400 c) 3.4
5 Answers will vary.

11 BLAST FROM THE PAST QUIZ
1 a) Santos
  b) Sevilla, Newell's Old Boys
  c) Liverpool
2 Pelé
3 a) 43 b) 47 c) 4
4 899
5 a) 106, 112 b) 112, 142
  c) 109, 136

13 WORLD CUP QUIZ
1 1999, 2007
2 Uruguay 2 times
  Italy 4 times
  West Germany 3 times
  Brazil 5 times
  England 1 time
  Argentina 2 times
  France 1 time
  Spain 1 time
3 15 goals
4 Here are the missing numbers in the chart.

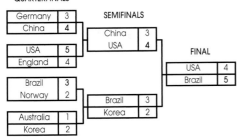

5 Brazil won the tournament.

15 LEAGUES QUIZ
1 League table after Week 5

	P	W	D	L	F	A	GD	PTS
1 City	5	3	2	0	8	5	+3	11
2 United	5	2	1	2	7	5	+2	7
3 Rovers	5	2	1	2	8	8	0	7
4 Rangers	5	0	2	3	2	7	-5	2

2 2nd United; 3rd Rovers
3 League table after Week 6

	P	W	D	L	F	A	GD	PTS
1 City	6	4	2	0	9	5	+4	14
2 Rovers	6	3	1	2	11	9	+2	10
3 United	6	2	1	3	7	6	+1	7
4 Rangers	6	0	2	4	3	10	-7	2

4 Rovers
5 1st City, 2nd Rovers,
  3rd United, 4th Rangers

17 SOCCER RIVALS QUIZ
1 a) 11 b) 4 c) 8
2 Real Madrid 86
  Barcelona 76
3 63 fans won't get in
4 30,787 spare places
5 8–4, 6–6

19 SOCCER STARS QUIZ
1 Cristiano Ronaldo, 261 days
2 Wayne Rooney
3 a) 323
  b) 315
4 a) 2004–2005 b) 2007–2008
  c) 2005–2006
5 Cristiano Ronaldo, 9 goals

21 BRAZIL QUIZ
1 Your table should look like this:

	P	W	D	L	F	A	GD	PTS
Brazil	3	3	0	0	8	3	+5	6
England	3	2	0	1	2	1	+1	4
Romania	3	1	0	2	4	5	-1	2
Czechoslovakia	3	0	0	3	2	7	-5	0

2 19
3 Two hundred ten
4 a) 9 $\frac{1}{2}$ b) 95 c) –8
  d) 190
5 a) True b) True c) False
  d) False e) True f) True

23 STADIUMS QUIZ
1 Rungrado May Day Stadium, Salt Lake Stadium, Estadio Azteca
2 25,189 (Red Bull Arena)
  82,238 (Estádio do Maracanã)
  83,500 (Stadium Australia)
  90,000 (Wembley Stadium)
  94,700 (Soccer City)
  105,000 (Estadio Azteca)
  120,000 (Salt Lake Stadium)
  150,000 (Rungrado May Day)
3 20,000
4 a) $\frac{2}{6}$ or $\frac{1}{3}$ b) $\frac{3}{6}$ or $\frac{1}{2}$
  c) $\frac{4}{6}$ or $\frac{2}{3}$
5 a) 40,000 b) 60,000 c) 80,000

25 SOCCER MONEY QUIZ
1 $141.66 million
2 $159.66 million
3 $50.86 million
4 Here are two combinations:
  Figo, Vieri, Shearer $131.48 million
  Kaká, Vieri $137.66 million
  How many others can you find?
5 A (red bar) Kaká
  B (yellow bar) Vieri
  C (blue bar) Zidane
  D (orange bar) Shearer
  E (green bar) Figo
  F (purple bar) Denilson

27 TRAINING QUIZ
1 7 $\frac{1}{2}$ hours
2 270 minutes
3 39 hours
4 1 $\frac{1}{2}$ hours (90 minutes)
5 a) Angle a is an acute angle; Angle b is an obtuse angle
  b) 90°; right angle
  c) 45°
  d) 150°

29 PRACTICE MAKES PERFECT QUIZ
1 a) 165 ft b) 99 ft c) 198 ft
  d) 132 ft
2 a) 1,056 ft b) 65,340 sq ft
3 (3,4) (4,5)
4 a) (4,3) (3,4)
  b) Yes
5 a) (4,2) (1,3) (2,2) (1,4)
  b) (1,4) (4,5)

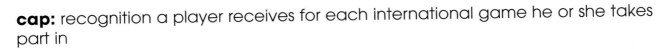
cap: recognition a player receives for each international game he or she takes part in

capacity: the number of people that there is room for

coordinate: any of a set of numbers used to tell the location of a point on a grid

defender: a player whose job is to prevent the other team from scoring

diagram: a drawing that shows the arrangement of something

goalkeeper: the player who defends the goal. Also called the goalie.

grid: a network of evenly spaced lines running across and up and down

intercept: to stop or interrupt the progress of

midfielder: one of the players who plays in the midfield, which is the part of the field midway between the two goals

perimeter: the distance around a 2D shape

pitch: playing field

referee: the top official in administering a game

sequence: a series

side: team

squad: team

stadium: a large building with raised rows of seats for viewers at sporting events

statistics: a collection of facts in the form of numbers

striker: a player who is striking or trying to strike the ball

timetable: schedule

winger: a team member who plays on one side of the center position

World Cup: the biggest international competition in soccer. The finals are held every four years.